FORMS OF PROTEST

Hannah Silva is a writer and theatre-maker whose work often starts from a playful interrogation of language, voice and form. As a poet she has performed at the Tokyo Design Centre, Krikri International Festival of Polyphony in Belgium, Poetry Hearings in Berlin and throughout the UK.

Her work for theatre includes the solo show *Opposition*, a play for a large cast of teenage girls, *Orchid*, and *The Disappearance of Sadie Jones*. She has written for radio and regularly appears on BBC Radio 3. Her latest play, *Gagged*, was a runner-up in the Leslie Scalapino Award for Innovative Women Playwrights. She is an associate lecturer in poetry and playwriting at Birkbeck College, University of London.

hannahsilva.co.uk

Forms of Protest

Hannah Silva

Penned in the Margins

LONDON

PUBLISHED BY PENNED IN THE MARGINS
Toynbee Studios, 28 Commercial Street, London E1 6AB
www.pennedinthemargins.co.uk

First published 2013

Printed in the United Kingdom by Bell & Bain Ltd.

ISBN
978-1-908058-17-1

CONTENTS

Acknowledgements

Some of these poems, or earlier versions, have appeared in the following publications: *Ink, Sweat & Tears, Tears in the Fence, Great Works, The Pedestal, Dear World & Everyone In It* (Bloodaxe Books, 2013), *Adventures in Form* (Penned in the Margins, 2012) and *Seductive Harmonies: the Poetry of Music* (Avalanche Books, 2012).

'Opposition' is an extract from the solo show of the same name, supported by Arts Council England and Apples and Snakes; 'Mannequin' was written on the Aldeburgh Jerwood Opera Writing Foundation Scheme and was composed by Joanna Lee and directed by Tom Creed; 'The Plymouth Sound' was originally commissioned by Paines Plough and the Drum Theatre Royal Plymouth for *Come To Where I'm From*; 'In the beginning' was commissioned by Theatre Bristol as a sound piece for *34 Bristols*.

Forms of Protest

for Nana, with love

In the beginning

in the beginning in the beginning in the beginning in the beginning

and the earth

was without
    was without

and the earth

and the
  and

and the earth   was without God
and the earth   was without Form
and the earth   was without Light
and the earth   was without Face

and the void the darkness the face the face

The face of the waters
            in the midst of the waters
        and let it divide
    the waters
            from the waters

Under the firmament

Above the firmament
and it was so

and God called the light 'day'
and God called the form 'deep'
and God called the void 'face'
and there was light/light the first day

and God saw Good and God said:

'Divide the waters from the waters
and the morning and the evening and the day'
                    and the day and the day

'Divide the waters

          from the waters

and let the waters gather

                    in one place'

It was so —

and god was without face
and god was without form
and god was without light
and god was the face the face
the darkness the face the face

Dry /Land /Good /Fruit /Kind /Seed /Grass /Herb /So/Earth
   ... *gathering gathering*

and the morning
and the evening
and the day

     and the earth
       and the god
         and the earth
    god was without face

and God   the Face of the divide
so kind so void

and it was
there was
was it?

and it was so
     so   *dry*
     so

Let the seasons be seasons let the signs be seasons/
   Let the seasons be signs for days and years and it was so

and divide the light
god/
seeds/

fruit/
so earth
let the waters gather
in one place   *gathering, gathering*

And god made light to rule the day
and lesser light to rule the night
and stars also

And rule over the day
And rule over the night
And divide the light
from the dark
  and God it was good
     and the evening and the morning and the day

And God said:
     'waters moving creatures life and foul fly and earth open'

(and the creature winged good and move)

'Be fruitful fly and multiply and fill the waters and the sky'

and the earth
and the evening
and the morning
and the fifth day

Hello My Friend

I am contacting you with something urgent,
you have always been a good friend
I need to inform you of the following:
It is important that we remain connected,
it is important we don't avoid the subject.
Please switch on your TV and watch the news.

Nothing happens in the world that isn't in the news,
nothing happens in the news that isn't urgent,
nothing happens until there is an urgent subject
and I would not be contacting you my friend,
if it wasn't for the importance of remaining connected,
if it wasn't that so many are following.

There is perhaps something sinister about following
with such attentiveness the many faces of the news.
Sometimes I wonder if we really need to be connected
to an idea, a chink in history that only now is urgent.
I wonder why I feel the need for a friend
when friendship has become a meaningless subject.

Yet I am asking you to stand alongside me on the subject,
I ask you to confess that we have been following
the instructions of a face we both called a friend
and I ask you to smile with me as we state that the news
of this latest update is a shock and that retraction is urgent
and we celebrate the fact that minds have connected.

There was a time when people became connected
when we connected them, became subject
when we subjected them, their ideas were never urgent
until we believed them. They followed and kept following,
we told our stories and our stories became news.
Keep dancing and you will always have a friend.

I understand the world through faces I call friends,
every day I ensure to remain connected.
There are many sources from which I glean news,
in the space above my thoughts I leave 'no subject'.
There are hundreds of people who are following
my brief statements and their replies are always urgent.

Hello my dear friend there is no subject no winning numbers
I am keeping you connected and I am following you,
I've told you the good news and now await your urgent respond.

Arvo Crash

He screams – she swears @ him.
There's Ø movN ndoors.

d c@ breathn on my gut.
A =o&o> zooms past,

a wmn on d bac S laffin.
d k9 S curled ^ on hs bed.

We're ll jst breathn. d 5-o siren
blaring as it pushes thru d traFK.

Calm dwn, dey sA 2 ea oder.
owtsd a CAB drivS past.

I'm nt movN. d tv S off
It's alw off n d daytime,

bt I'm nt calm. coz it's me –
d centA of ll dis. I'm d Ntrtamnt.

3 o'clock n d arvo, d tym I alw fall |-I.
IK I'm n my car. I read,

put dwn d b%k n DSapER.
I can't Xpln – my bod doesn't

seem lk my bod, it feels as f
4 hrs n sumtyms it S.

My lgz don't feel lk my lgz,
my arms don't feel lk my arms.

d animals r zzz.

A Second

rises and dissipates word
for emotion throat sudden
goes a word for emotion rises
sudden welling goes and

dissipates. A second should
be a word that rises and
disappears a sudden wailing
through the throat emotion for a word
wilting in a second

throat should appear dissipate
in a sudden veiling should be a word
rising in motion and the world is patient
or hidden in a word for the notion
should be suddenly paled.

Is there a word for emotion
that rises for a second
and dissipates? A sudden
welling in the throat and it goes.

A mo ina _/ jar

f I cUd capture a mo
I'd av done it by now, I'd B
hovering, an Austin pwrs kinda
img, ina _/ ful of mist.
That's w@ we cllD it –
d tyms we weren't blind
bac frm d pub stumble
he spoke as f he'd raped me
n d tree's branchs brushd
agenst us 4 a mo. d 2 men s@
cYd by cYd n 1of em replayd
d tyms we couldn't DsciB,
lyN bac on d grass n fallN
N2 it, fallN deep so d oder mn
z, m8 she's yrz. Go gt her.
Go gt her m8. &he did.
Didn't you? As f dat wz it,
dat simpl. u thort, 1day n d
fucha der wl B a _/ jar on a
countA ina rm dat l%ks lk
u n l%ks lk M2 n dat jar wl
contain ll deez moments,
n d mist swirls arnd em,
n we'll sumhw B preserved.

Gaddafi Gaddafi Gaddafi

I am not going to tell you my name Gaddafi but I am
going to tell you my age Gaddafi my age is ten
Gaddafi and I am going to tell you about a game
Gaddafi a game that I play Gaddafi I play with my
friends Gaddafi you can play it alone Gaddafi
or play it with friends Gaddafi. Go into a room

Gaddafi a room with strong walls
Gaddafi strong floor and strong ceiling
Gaddafi and choose a word Gaddafi not any word
Gaddafi but carefully Gaddafi you carefully choose
Gaddafi an immense word Gaddafi with immense meaning
Gaddafi with immense meaning to you Gaddafi
Gaddafi and with your friends Gaddafi all together
Gaddafi together you chant Gaddafi you chant that word
Gaddafi over and over Gaddafi Gaddafi over and over.

We chose a word Gaddafi we chose this word
'Gaddafi' we chant: Gaddafi Gaddafi Gaddafi
over and over Gaddafi Gaddafi Gaddafi
together Gaddafi Gaddifi Gaddafi
loudly Gaddafi Gaddafi Gaddafi all through
Gaddafi the night Gaddafi and through Gaddafi
the day Gaddafi the Gaddafi night the Gaddafi day:
Gaddafi Gaddafi Gaddafi. Other words might be quicker

Gaddafi but this word Gaddafi this word takes longer
Gaddafi Gaddafi. We stay in the room with
strong walls strong floor strong ceiling Gaddafi
Gaddafi for day after day after day Gaddafi
Gaddafi week after week after week Gaddafi
Gaddafi until Gaddafi at last Gaddafi one morning
Gaddafi one morning the word is the same

as all other words gaddafi gaddafi and we keep on
chanting gaddafi gaddafi gaddafi until the word loses
its meaning completely gaddafi and we keep on chanting
gaddafi gaddafi gaddafi we chant our way through this
loss of meaning until we become a gaddafi of horses
galloping: *gaddafi gaddafi gaddafi.*

The Periphery

Silt it, sweetheart — said with a lilt and a head to one side,
fag-end between builder's fleshy stubs — we're still squabbling
over going to the city.
I explain about the walls with bullet holes,
shrapnel embedded in pavements.
Memories don't just wash,
no one's fault, but I can't seem to clip clip clip
my way clock clock clock my heels across broken glass.
I want to put myself in his pocket and
worry about our inability to explain the absence of black holes
from the darkness.
You see, I am a replica.
It's only an abortion.
I don't know if I am being fractious; I don't know what it means
to be honest.
But we are splintering and I am cautious and threatened
and I think we are going to fracture –
to separate, fracture.
Is that what you want?
Frankly yes, to be separate.
Separated from, separate to.
Smoking kills, killing all of us.
Walking away. Have a lovely day.

The Riverbank

She didn't know what it meant
when she walked through the city of the rich
and no one touched her, except physically.

What do you do with a slut?
Reach for the ketchup bottle.

Go back to the riverbank where the swans were
sleeping before they were hurt by the edges,
the dream's actual edges.

She is simply walking a street
identity burning between legs — she takes a piece
of broken glass, her saliva is dead water.

All the kisses join up, like tears on a window
forming bridges she learns how to speak.

She holds a gun in her hand, she wishes
she held a gun in her hand.

You will leave behind an immensely human smell.

The Citadel

Shadows are unpinned from us
and roam between the traffic, slipping
into new skins. They own these humans.
Yes we are living — slightly.

Years ago the squid from Plymouth Sound
were massive, brought back to the lab to be
examined then tossed over a shoulder, landing
on the ceiling and staying there — stuck, suckers.

The parrot was left in the library
when they went down to the tunnels.
This is not the future we are talking about,
simple bombing, simply bang bangs.

When I see an image I see a lamp
light along a corridor called history,
stumbling, echoes patched back
together, there's a sound.

Paintings of stick figures on the walls,
arms up — surrender or success?
There must be a finish line ahead.
The face is a gas mask or a snail shell.

I know, I know — ghosts ghost ghosts

are still dancing, still dancing.
Anyway, they say we're winning so
shush — young ones — shush.

Hyas Araneus

All animals have a minimum space requirement
without which survival is impossible.

Bubbles overlap, social animals
need to stay in touch, it varies species to species.

The critical distance is so precise
it can be measured in centimeters.

The English have characteristically demonstrated
that they are not afraid to plan.

In the spring, each male stickleback
carries out a circular territory.

Social distance in man has been extended
by telephone, TV and the walkie-talkie.

In the cold waters of the North sea
lives a form of crab, *Hyas Araneus*.

At certain times in the life cycle,
the individual becomes vulnerable to others.

Do we grasp because we have hands
or do we have hands because we grasp?

Crabs are solitary crustaceans.
This is 1966. Look at the advantages

held by those that have a territory, a space
of their own. Look at the advantages.

The Plymouth Sound

He was a poet. She was a musician. He writes her a letter. It's about a dream: The Citadel, a parrot, the sea, tunnels, soldiers running past.

Sitting with her back to him, music in the distance, a young French woman listens, tiny fingers, playing. I was a poet and you were a musician.

Sometimes I don't remember your name. 'Leave the parrot in the library.' The bombs just keep falling; the city is in flames

on this dead city, inside this scooped out throat of a city with nothing but air passing through, wind rushing through. He can't play anymore, she watches. What are you looking at? Soldiers running past.

It's not easy to talk about a place when you've forgotten its name. It's not easy to read my father's handwriting. What happened? It's hard to speak. The fingers stop working, the articulations stop articulatingtktktktktk... and the piano in the distance goes quiet.

'Leave the parrot in the library and come with me.' Listen: bang bang. 'Leave the piano in the distance and.' I imagine you reading this letter on the — what do you call it? Looking at the water. He studied biology at Oxford.

Grey boats grey water grey clouds. There's no difference between the water and the sky. It's not so hard Dad, stop complaining, just taste the words, find the sounds again, let's just watch the Sound together.

It definitely does start with a letter. He played Bach. Ae ah oh er ae. He said my fingers were too tiny, he sat in Darwin's library, to play the piano. Oh er ih ah ee. He called it his Citadel. Sometimes I don't remember your name.

In his dream she was sitting with her back to him, the young French woman, then she pressed her breasts against his face: smooth and warm and unreal and real and sickening sickening sickening... Dad! I don't think that's the kind of thing... you should tell me about whispering and sounds.

You used to play Bach, and... inappropriate laughter. He was a poet and I was... The whole city in flames... What do you do without names? He had a parrot. Blue and red.

The first letter he's ever written, it does appear to be him talking. We used to play together. He is a musician and I am...

His daughter, reading his first letter. We used to play Bach together. Strange things to dream about.

'Just leave the bloody parrot in the library and come with me.' He told me I was shouting 'leave the bloody parrot and...'

There's a tiny metal door in the brain and it's impossible to open, it's impossible to collect to re to recollect the names intertwined it must be nice to see the sea.

In his brain was a blood clot like a treble clef. I was crying and he was sitting with his back to me. He doesn't remember my name. It doesn't matter. I was a musician and you were a poet. Is that right?

Or was it the other way around? His fingers are still strong. She was a poet, he was a musician. It's just patterns, it's just sound. I didn't understand how to describe a dream that he had.

There was a piano, a parrot in the library, books filled with Darwin's drawings and a French woman, bombing, soldiers, lost names, music in the distance. He couldn't remember exactly. Dust... there was a library, drawings, the sea and soldiers running past.

I went to the library in the laboratory on Citadel Hill. A young French woman sat with her back to me and listened. 'There was a parrot here,' she said. 'They would leave it in the library during the bombing, they'd go down into the tunnels. Can you hear the piano... in the distance... beneath the Citadel?'

As I read his letter, I can hear him playing Bach. I decide to tell him it was on Citadel Hill, in this city... his dream is some kind of memory.

'Where is it you live again?' He asks. 'I'm sure it begins with P.' Don't worry, I tell him. I can't remember, it doesn't matter.

Translations

I
salt la la pale bra

aid lent deal pen same into
aid lent deal sun I do
la la pale bra salt a comb in cab hallo
aid lent deal Vienna too
comb over nun no villa do a zoo free
aid lent den lain no chain
see pier vapour call yes dare me crane yo
in toads parts loss who yeahs deign fine
in lain car a deli tore eons ill tatters Odin hello
in ill sex oh deign lain eagles ill tattoo aye electric
suss patters into cool cruel says senile violette
ill torn a soul quell girl
haste ill blank
haste ill grit haste ill pleasure

II
Salted pale girl singing la la la

Lend me a pen and I'll deal the same
I'll deal the sun I do.
She wears a pale bra singing la la la
salting a comb through her hair.

Hailing a cab with a hello lo lo
all the way to Vienna's aid,
and the nun with a comb over rents her a villa
a free zoo a lone den with no chains.

III

I lay down in the lion's den without chains,
you can see the pier from here, the vapour pours
over call the deal off yes towards all the parts of loss,
the design is fine. Alone in the car, an eagle
tore over my back like Odin in tatters it's been
aeons since this illness, the electric tattoo
on my sex where the bird of prey lay eye it patters
on skin into cruel senile violence, too cool,
too torn her soul to quell the girl, haste back
the illness blanks the grit of haste, the pleasure.

IV
Finish the word

Until the thought is thinking
until the sound
the word stops like a horse
facing the wind
as if a new image of suffering
continues through the night

sulfurous he's lost in the streets of my mind
every part of us is in the fire
there's a tree like a tattoo across the face
the wind tattoos the air
an electric tattoo in the sex of the church
in some of us and in you
in parts of us as you exhale
the summer violence the sunflower
the tornado comes until blankness
until the grit until the end.

Holding

Hold your nerve, your kneecaps have not slipped
yet.

Hold you nerve, your back doesn't make you cry
yet.

How old you our nervous you are new you our
toy.

Hold your nerve, it doesn't hurt to breathe
yet.

Old who you are our verve is your revere
get.

Hold your nerve, the twinges are not continuous
yet.

Fold our reverie in your hold how you verse us
yes.

Hold your nerve, you're not an old woman
yet.

Yet our refrain our hollow are versus your hour
olds.

School of Music

We ran down corridors at night, screaming and laughing,
arriving at the bathroom where a susurrus of arias
haunted us — the singers' favourite practice cell.

Counting pills with no knickers, she sits on the edge
of the sofa, legs open. She's Korean, we'd say,
and this explained it all — the insanity, the sex.

He ran across the grass at night, out of the dew-dark
into my bed. This is intense, this living together.
He was never inside me for long.

I ran into myself one night, escaped at dawn, on the Circle Line
alone. I ran back to let his sweetness cancel out the other.
Come over scum. Obliterate or save. I forgave myself.

It rang in the corridor at night, two notes for one — home.
Please leave a message after the long B flat.
All along the wall someone had scrawled: 'I Hate Exeat.'

Running up an escalator Sara says: 'Let's just not eat.'
I reply: 'Let's go get something pierced.'
In the morning I'll cry into my bath, but now it's night,

and she puts down *The Pelican Brief* and we toast
to red hair, law, and no more cello. With drunken

eyes we improvise seduction in a mirror.

Only our reflections run into each other so it isn't real —
the white towelled dressing gowns,
the boys listening outside the door,

the black pubic hair against creamy skin,
the impossibility of orgasm,
the half-heartedness of this performance.

Her sex didn't speak to me, but it didn't hurt;
it didn't give or take but at least it was easy.
Afterwards, I remember thinking —
man or woman, it doesn't matter, but there has to be love.

The Bride

everyone's happy nowadays
mother refers to her body
her wing shadows

swallow mother
carry mother

everyone's useful nowadays
it is it is virgin unfolded language
this idle child

makes tragedy
drinks tragedy

everyone makes sense
this dream is
a foreign substance   protest

a myth a rose she is everyone
she makes shapes

in her mother's shoes
cruelty vanishes
hideous hideous hide us

our usefulness
single teardrops

The Empty House

Writing to someone else's music, I predict my own. It opens between notes; it licks, it licks, it likes the sound in a cell the piano next door, everyone flees.

In a derelict momentum we travel across bridges. A serpent and another empty house. An inside out, the belongings reveal

They reveal a body working in spite of itself. A fake sun on leaves. How did we leave these flakes of ourselves so visible? So visible.

Look at him run. He is sweat, thigh, dust, cries. Look at his eyes. Cry their found look, his eyes look found. In his tears his running beats.

What about your music? The streets fall behind and and

What are you doing? Why are you here? What's that noise? I'm walking towards you. I've been here since yesterday. Will you photograph me naked? This is my perfect. Will you watch me forever? My perfect kindness. Have me.

You looked different yesterday. This is my shiver on a repeating dream playing on a grand piano while the disintegration surrounds

Will the torn sound repent? All the tears touch each other. They like to be touched. This is someone else's disease shared she he here descend end end

Look at the dust. Look how smooth the mark is left. Look how the traces match the waiting costs. I think this is like whispering to friends who listen tight. The sounds at night, the sounds at night.

Insults

You are a multitasking muppit
You are a new age mini me
You are a no-brainer monkey
You are a down and dirty diva
You are a surreal pandemic
You are an uber wacky
You are a poor man's metaphor
You are an immortal waste of space
You are a water cooler moment
You are a doomsday scenario
You are a coping mechanism
You are a trophy wife
You are a textbook squeeze
You are an appalling cock-up
You are award-winning car-crash TV
You are not a happy bunny
You are a low-rent loser
You are a challenged cubicle monkey
You are a cash cow
You are a low fat drizzle
You are a pan-fried postmodernist
You are a learning curve
You are a bubbly mindset

Blank the in

died I last at until eyes open wide   with water under swam   I bathe the in   turn my replied I   line overused an   ask to left nothing   kisses less self less my tongue my language   lost it   down it wrote   it lost sex having

time in   space in travel to   wanted   dislocated   felt I bed in   the in the side   the out thought slide thin the lost slice   feel like flesh ultra rubber expensive most the blend exclusive an   breasts my offered I special felt it but unusual not   watched man a

up woke laughter salted slaughter tasted water wasted daughter taste of I   happiness of moments brief in emotion: thought I   sex changing imagined   text by will my sent   a great massacre has been there   completely a me made complete me made I thinking by just beginning the in

in the Blank

in the beginning just by thinking I made me complete made me a completely   there been has massacre great a   sent my will by text imagined changing sex   I thought: emotion in brief moments of happiness I of taste daughter wasted water tasted slaughter salted laughter woke up

a man watched not unusual but it felt special   I offered my breasts an exclusive blend the most expensive rubber ultra flesh like feel slice lost the thin slide thought out the side the in the   in bed I felt dislocated   wanted   to travel in space in time

having sex   lost it wrote it down it lost   language my tongue my less self less kisses   nothing left to ask   an overused line I replied my turn   in the bath I   swam under water with   wide open eyes until at last I died

@Prosthetics

Twenty percent of those with prosthetic
limbs will go back into war #apositivething

A little girl cuts the arm off and the eye
out of her doll #apositivething

Amputation is the first step
in rehabilitation #apositivething

'It looks like a monster now,' she says
just like her father #apositivepositivepositivething

Mannequin

1

Summer

Summer's a breeze in an easy wear wardrobe of florals and brightly coloured silks!

Su Mm m mmmm m m er er er's a br eeeeeee ea sy breee zy lemon squeeeeee zy eeeeze ease

 pierce burn tease freeze

 Stitch it split it nip it zip it perfect fit

 Change is: Good! Ooooo!

Ease easy w ear ward   d d d drape dip dye to die for robe of fl peek pinch it tuck it poke it perfect

 Change is GGGGG!
orals and f f f f f florals b
right
ly colou red slick silks Ultra fem inine

 Yes!
 pretty Oh so pretty Change! titty titty titty

tacky plas nervous tic plas tic drastic fantastic
stick ch ch Change Yes Ange el l l l

Ohsoohsoohsoohsoohso
Ohsoohsoohsooh

pop pull fry paint scoop

per fectperf ectperfe ctperfec tperfect perfectdefectinfectreflect

Oh so perfect!

2

Autumn

Put on a brave face. Anti-girlie blush. Pout with punch. Look at me liner.
Sultry smack. Vamp it up. Come hither eyes. Yes!

fa cial lost face save facelift faceoff face deface erase face facts face it

Your g uide   our your guided guide us

   Your guide to
Autumn's!

         fall flaw less sell us! Sed   uctive loooks oooo Sed
ative

farcical flay soft faze fave force

Change! Efface! Bold!

smile s s s split spill slip lip tears tears ears chic cheek
   eyes Yes! nose No!

face deface erase deface erase efface

This season's look is
                Faceless!

3

Winter

*She photographs extraordinarily well to the point of actually seeming
alive. Even without the face it's easy to imagine her personality!*

We sa sa s say save sell
lute win t   in
ter's eleg   her
ant mili   m military military
tary inspired   inspire expire sp sp
suicide   redd eadp erfectin fectde fectre flect
smock   suicideinsidesmockmock

      Scoop Neck   sc oooo k
      V Neck   v n k
      Halter Neck   Ha ha ha k k k t
      Bateau Neck   eau eau t t t t k k
      Boat Neck   b b bow row boat gently   n k
      Cowl Neck   l l merrily!
      Crew Neck
      No neck
      neck and neck lace
      necklace
      neck   breath less
      less   neck less
      Decollette

4

Spring

She is a very popular mannequin. Durable. Affordable. Natural. White matt finish.

less man I mate quin ult oice oice f f f lex

> Height:
> 1550 millimetres

lexibilequins de d less

> Bust:
> 830 millimetres

less mann e quins are the ult I mate

> Waist:
> 630 millimetres

ch ch ch oice f f or flex ibility

> Hips:
> 880 millimetres

head the ult I mate ch ch ch choice f f lexibil titty t t t t t t

Base diameter
1.380 millimetres

choice less the ultimate sni uq enn am
sniuqennam mannequins flex less

Head
Less

Headless mannequins are the ultimate choice for flexibility!

Bone Ladder

I was speaking just to clean that woman
in a bone woman ladder just speaking to
a bone in that clean woman
[*whisper*] that woman I was just
speaking to she climbed
a bone ladder in clean skin

She _has_in_her_veins a massive   coming out t t t t t t t t a naked turning
in =to blank in to= catalogue_blood_moments   moments

_catalogue life moments
_in order to
_an infinity of
_category until

a library of bodies unread   did you want to touch?

On the other side of the make, the victims extend their wounds and
ripple slowly up for surface listening; drinking nakwine

We are drinking nakwine!
Sitting in dead arm chairs
Until hallucinations subside

transform the nak   ed   wine   to FORM the for the WILD form the form the naked WINE to form the trans naked TO transform the naked wine to wild

garlic while we close our eyes and type wearing white gloves

ty-pe-de ty-pe-pe ty-pe-de ty-pe-pe ty-pe ty-pe tight hang   cast
line   side

can we show our hands?
creature, retreat
now_swallow the waiting in quiet.

Popocatépetl

Acrobatic children in many colours
piled up like fruit at the market,
we are afraid to touch, afraid to taste,
as if there is some magic to poverty, as if
on the stroke of reality, it disappears.
A cinematic ciudad, with volcanoes
keeping it in, Mexico is made of
morning and night, atole and tequila.
We play a game of underground
Pictionary and map each day,
each holiday; Christmas Eve
would not be the same without a child
somersaulting over her mother's
body in front of our car, at midnight.

Le Momo

I wish to die holding my boots
following a session on a block of wood:
scream, gasp, thwack, cry, laugh, clap
my daughters are watching, my friends
join in with an axe. We spit and belch in
rhythmic patterns until instruments of
our hearts find harmonics, overtones —
Over night we make a new language
then at the crossroads we are abandoned
by all possible human feeling.
I blow you a raspberry: tsk tsk tsk —
Simply to settle on a truth, one with a single
edge, no forked tongue. There are few of us
who have really tried to get a hold on things,
to create within ourselves spaces for that which
does not exist. I wind up my breath for this:
the clockwork of the soul.

Tory Party Sonnet

There are no women left, can't win
carpeted halls, a place that smelt, women left
exhausted sandwiches spoke only to themselves.
There are some women, it is true, small numbers,
bright colours, women are subject to its agitated
measures the women are left there explicitly
told them to calm down so poverty women left
no women left 'sexless' there is worse to come —
Wearing a pearl ear-ring, the stage woman leaves
photographers maps and shovels, a swift belly rub
with a kind of wonky pride and a chunk of Wonga
contempt, no women there, edges glow red.
The women are left to dust or ice-cream;
They like the word, but misunderstand its meaning.

New Orleans

In a room above the streets he paints.
He paints a corpse on the ground
and a musician on a rooftop. He dips his brush
into water and sees dead bodies, floating
to the surface. He remembers that someone
once said: 'God help us.' In his lost mind, politicians
cut the throats of babies. A helicopter doesn't stop,
with a brush stroke, he sends the cop to hell.
In a dab of white paint a bunch of flowers falls —
hangs suspended, gravity abandoned
adorns a mass grave while a woman sings:
Yo soy la desintegración

He wants to touch her. He knows that after this
there is no more contact, no more belief.

Rest in Peace

The world is just coming to us, just coming to us now.

Murdering pregnant one year-old, voices
in her head and the trial both. And the trial
and the trial trial trial trial trial trial both

died, knife into her back, casually walking.
Walking away now walking away walking
walking away now walking. Hello!

Fairly warm day into the weekend too some
sunshine in the east. Intrusive restrictive freedom
rolls is the state becoming too? Intrusive

restrict our freedom roll back the boundaries a big
bang approach transform our politics far less control
over less less control over more more control over

less less control over more over less holes in that cloud
still a chance of a spot or two of rain it really will feel
very pleasant. Hand power back to the people we can

build a fair society. I'll be back in half an hour to save
the world's smallest water lily (which is obviously what
we're waiting for) after her stabbing at the end of last
week and on her car it says: 'rest in peace'.

Opposition

Extracts from a political play on words

I

It's great to be here in Liverpool
we're happy about that.
I've been in Downing Street
it's great to be here in Liverpool.
We're happy about Downing Street
it's great to be here in Liverpool.

II

It's my hope and my mission
that the business of government falls
it seems to me into two categories.

The government falls it goes without saying
into categories.

The government falls
The government falls
The government fools
Different sorts of fools
Different sorts of ideas

Two categories:
One, two do do do do do do

There are the things you do
The things you do
You do the things
Sometimes unpopular
The things you do
It's your duty
National interest
We're happy about that.

And yes cutting the
And yes cutting the nat
And yes cutting the national

And yes cutting the cutting the cutting cutting
the cutting cutting cutting cutting cutting cutting
cutting cutting cutting cutting cutting cutting cutting
cuttingcuttingcuttingcuttingcuttingcuttingcuttingcctctctctctct
tcctctctctctctctctctctctctctctctctctctctctctctctctctctctctctctctcYes

Cutting the national deficit
Falls into that camp
We're happy about that.

But then there are the things you do
The things you do
You do the things

You do things do you?
You do. You do big things
Big Big things
because it's your passion
The things that fire
that drive, that spur, that inspire
that you truly believe (in the mornings)
that make a real difference
to your mornings to your country
You love your mornings
You love your count —

III

My big passion is building the
My great passion is building the
My large passion is
My huge passion is build
My massive pass
My enormous colossal
astronomical monumental
cataclysmic ginormous
humongous passion is building the —

I can't tell you how excited I am
It's not a passing interest
it's an idea I spoke about when I ran

I ran I ran
Election Campaign   terrible mess
And when I stood   terrible terrible
I stood I stood   mess
On the steps of Street Downing   previous government
And today today today we   inherited inherit t t t t d d
And today I want to take   to explain   to take   to talk

And today
After all that talking
All that talking All that talking
All that talking All that talking
All that talking All that talking
talking talking talking talking
talking taking taking taking
tktktktktktktktktktktktktktktktk
talking talking talking talking
taking taking taking taking taking
We're finally doing.

And today   *A concerted all-out war on gangs and gang culture*
This opportunity (titty)
Call to arms   *Stamping out these gangs is a new national priority*
Real practical steps
Together we will build:

ER   IH   OH – AY – IH – EE

Why is it such a powerful idea?

You can call it liberalism
You can call it empowerment
You can call it freedom
You can call it responsibility (titty)
I call it: 'Er Ih Oh-ay-ih-ee'

Liberalism it can call
Empowerment call it call it
Freedom can it can it
Responsibility (titty) can
I call it: 'Er Ih Oh-ay-ih-ee'

In my very first act as leader
It's great to be here in Liverpool
I signalled my personal priority
Liverpool personal priority Liverpool
London personal priority to build
to mend to build to mend our br br
one nation k k... nation... our
b b our aspiration k k br br brok
nation our br br k k

ER OH – EH OH – AY – IH – EE

IV

What more do you want to be able to do?
People.

Different sorts of people.
People in their everyday 'people' lives
Their 'people' homes
Their 'people' neighbourhoods
Their 'people' workplace

Don't always turn to powerful enough problems they face local
or central businesses helping trained authorities setting schools
up great for work charities to rehabilitate local authorities to face
offenders liberation dramatic biggest power elite the elite man the
elite woman the street man the street woman the most dramatic
man the most dramatic womble

All of the above
Must now
Help Themselves

Come together
Work together
We're in this together!
Different and bold
And this is blindingly obvious
people people people
millions of people giving

their time their effort even
their money their money
your money your money
your money money money
money money money

V

We need to turn this government completely on its head.

VI

We have not hired a Tsar.

VII

Calm down dear.

VIII

Are you upper class or middle class?
I don't really buy these labels
Gun to my head, I suppose I'd describe myself as 'well off'.
I don't buy these class things because they're all going.
What do these labels mean any more?

IX

My Big Passion
The Biggest Budget Deficit
My Big Idea
The Biggest Past Decade
Big Britains
Big Uglies
Big enough and Bold enough
At our Best when at our Boldest
We Do Big Things
A Big Bang Approach
Bish Bash Bosh

X

Beggars belief
No holds barred
Full and frank discussion
Feel good factor
Eye on the ball
I'm not ruling anything out and I'm not ruling anything in
Knee jerk reaction
Elephant in the room
Hearts and minds
Lessons must be learned
I can't comment on individual cases
Doing nothing is not an option

Worst-case scenario
Nightmare scenario
Doomsday scenario
No comment
No easy answers
Rip roaring
Recipe for disaster
On message
Consider your position
Rights and responsibilities
The terrible mess we inherited
Ring-fence
Road map
Singing from the same hymn sheet
With respect!

XI

Yes, there will be objections
But you know what?
We're happy about that.

Trial

An adaptation of Franz Kafka's *The Trial*

I
Preface

Someone must have been telling lies about Josef K
One morning, he was arrested
A knock on the door and a man entered.

II
The Arrest

Who are you?
It's my thirtieth birthday — perhaps it's a joke
Why am I under arrest?
They don't answer questions like that
I don't know this law
That doesn't make me guilty!
I must make a telephone call to the state attorney
Very well I won't make the telephone call
No I don't want to anymore
Go to work as normal?
In that case it's not too bad, being under arrest.

The supervisor seems to be comparing the length of his fingers.
The supervisor puts on a hat using two hands.

III

Cross-examination

You should have been here one hour five minutes ago.
You should have been here one hour five minutes ago.

Well maybe I have arrived late, but I'm here now.
Now then, you are a house painter?
No, I am the chief clerk in a large bank.
Ten days ago I was placed under arrest.
The arrest itself is something I laugh about
but that is beside the point.
They came to me in the morning when I was still in bed.

It was my thirtieth
symptomatic start to finish
start to enquiry but let's
suppose that I do do — sh sh sh!
SSSH! I have nearly finished.
Please don't take notes.

You bunch of louts! You can keep all your hearings as a present from
me!

IV
The Lawyer

Defence is not really allowed under law
it is merely tolerated.
There is a hole in the floor
not large enough for a man to fall though
but if your foot goes through
it will hang down right in the corridor
where the accused are waiting.

What sort of acquittal do you want?
Absolute acquittal, apparent acquittal or deferment?

The first acquittal is followed by a second arrest
The second acquittal by the third arrest
The third acquittal by the fourth arrest
Fourth acquittal by the fifth arrest
Fifth acquittal six arrest
Six acquittal seventh arrest
Seventh acquittal eighth arrest
Eighth acquittal ninth arrest
Ninth acquittal tenth arrest
arrest arrest suh tuh
stuh a rest a rest zest
a a a a quit! All quit!
ittall it all it   all l l law
All quit all!

Perhaps a deferment would suit you better?
Would you like me to explain what deferment is about?
Leave the carpet alone and listen to what the lawyer is saying!

V

Nightmare

Can you not see two steps in front of you?
The court accepts you when you come and it lets you go
when you leave.

VI

Judgement

top hats
double chins
march together
six legged lifeless
        bridge
light
                moon
        water
quarry

lent against a stone

thin double edged
butcher's knife
    must take the knife

won't take the knife   glinting

where is the judge?
where is the high court?

push the knife deep
cheek by cheek
twist   close to face
watching

'Like a dog!' He said.

— it was as if the shame could outlive him.

An Egoistic Deed

A pleasant and polite man, just like you and me.
A gay male, a normal person, to speak with him,

to eat with him 'seeks youth of good build,
seeks hunk 18-30 to slaughter.'

He ate whilst reciting the 23rd Psalm. *Thou art with me.*
My nipples look forward to your stomach.

Thy rod and thy staff, they comfort me.
Nothing is so delicious. *Thou annointest my head.*

The most respectful way to eat the human body,
he remembered him with every piece of flesh he ate.

My cup runneth over. The prosecution, however
feels that these hobbies (though legal) are very dangerous.

It's hard to know if he planned to serve a penis that night
or if the idea came up once the two men were together.

Thank You and Good Bye

There's no easy way to say this:
we recorded history and we made history
and for that I am sorry.

Phones were hacked,
and for that you should apologise.

We made a pledge, we didn't stick to it
and for that this paper is truly sorry.

When we're wrong we hold our hands up
but when we're right '*I'm comfortable getting them out*'
we holds our heads up too.

Self-regulation *does* work
wham, bam… thank you glam.

But most of all, we'll miss YOU
and for that we are truly sorry.

Sharing Faces

its face is the face in the face of the face
    the door the bridges joining losing falling
tonight   scrawled backwards by a fisted
  internet search

its face is the face in the face of the face
  a flat packed city   unpacked
the baby balanced in its centre
      laughing   because we don't understand

its face is the face in the face of the face
    the air is ink blot   the night is scribbled
watch it smile   watch it worship   warship rosehip

its face is the face in the face of the face
  we must talk about faces
                     sharing

its face is the face in the face of the face
  of course I recognise that face

it is a lonely place
    the body stretched out across the river
        walk on it   I dare you

Notes

'Opposition' is indebted to David Cameron's 'Big Society' speech, Liverpool, 2010.

'An Egoistic Deed' works with the story of Armin Meiwes.

'Le Momo' is for Antonin Artaud and is indebted to his diaries.

'Thank You and Good Bye' borrows from Nick Clegg and *News of the World*.

'Translations' begins as a homophonic translation of an Octavio Paz poem 'Disparo'.

'The Riverbank' is for Kathy Acker.

'In the beginning' is inspired by the Reverend Callaway, pipe smoker and Baptist preacher, who believed he had discovered the original Garden of Eden in Bristol, Florida.

'Tory Party Sonnet' is indebted to Tanya Gold's article in the *Guardian*, 13th October 2012: 'The Tories can't win without women, so why the disdain?'